Guru Nanak

SRI JAPJI SAHIB

English translation from the original Gurmukhi

ਜਪੁਜੀ ਸਾਹਿਬ

Guru Nanak

"He who lowers his mind to the dust of all men's feet, Sees the Name of God enshrined in every heart."

--Guru Arjan

ਜਪੁਜੀ ਸਾਹਿਬ

Guru Nanak

SRI JAPJI SAHIB

English translation from the original Gurmukhi

Format Design by
David Christopher Lane

Mt. San Antonio College
Walnut, California

ਜਪੁਜੀ ਸਾਹਿਬ

Guru Nanak

SRI JAPJI SAHIB

Fourth Edition | Trade paperback

ISBN: 978-1-56543-235-2

MSAC *Philosophy Group* was founded in 1990 and is designed to provide a wide range of materials (from books to magazines to films to audio presentations to interactive texts) on such subjects as evolutionary biology, quantum theory, neuroscience, and critical studies in religion and philosophy. All books are sold on a not for profit basis. Free PDF versions are made available whenever possible. In addition, there is a growing collection of audio books specifically created for students at Mt. San Antonio College and the community at large. A large series of original movies have also been produced which touch on such topics as artificial intelligence, eliminative materialism, consciousness, and skepticism.

ਜਪੁਜੀ ਸਾਹਿਬ

INTRODUCTION

Although I am not a Sikh, I have long been deeply impressed by the teachings of Guru Nanak and his nine successors. Indeed, I believe that the *Sri Guru Granth Sahib*, the sacred writings of Sikhism, is unique amongst the world's religions. Not only does it contain the hymns of six of the Sikh gurus, but also of the Sant poets Kabir, Ravidas, and Namdev. The universal and eclectic nature of the *Sri Guru Granth Sahib* is perhaps best epitomized by its inclusion of poems by the revered Muslim mystic, Sheikh Farid.

When I was but eighteen years old, I chanced upon Gopal Singh's English translation of the *Sri Guru Granth Sahib* at the now defunct bookstore, Bodhi Tree, in West Hollywood. Beautifully bound in a special four-volume set, I immediately wanted to buy it but the price was prohibitive for me at that time. It was 80 dollars. Having already read excerpts from Guru Nanak's beautiful teachings, I was determined to read the entire holy book. So I saved money from my job as a "box boy" at the local market and within a couple of weeks bought the entire set. Nearly forty-five years later I still own this treasured possession.

The *Sri Japji Sahib* was composed by Guru Nanak and is the opening prayer of the *Sri Guru Granth Sahib.* It is widely regarded as containing the heart of Sikh teachings.

Sri Japji Sahib was first published in Gurmukhi in 1604. There are now several English translations of the text, but nothing can compare to actually listening to it sung aloud when visiting the exquisite Golden Temple of the Sikhs in Amritsar, Punjab, India.

I have visited the Golden Temple several times, but my most memorable experience was in

March 21st of 2017 when my family and I got the privilege of visiting the sacred center at night. In the essay, "Devotional Thickness: The Sacredness of Human Longing," specially written for *Integral World* in Europe, I explain what transpired: I didn't expect to be overwhelmed with emotion and I certainly didn't expect to be transformed by the experience. But there I was witnessing something quite astonishing, and right in the midst of it a long forgotten book title by C.S. Lewis came to the forefront of my mind-- *Surprised by Joy*. The atmosphere was electric, but what struck me most forcefully was the unconditional love that permeated the surroundings. It was on the night of March 21, 2017, and I wanted to see the holiest of Sikh Gurdwaras, the Golden Temple. My family and I had just arrived in Amritsar in the Punjab just a few hours prior on Vistara Airlines from Delhi. I was in India conducting research for a new project for Oxford University Press and only had 12 or so hours before having to travel to Beas. Although I had first visited the Golden Temple in the summer of 1978 (which, coincidentally was also connected with a research project on the same subject), I had never seen it at night.

I knew that the surrounding area had been dramatically renovated and that the Golden Temple had become increasingly popular as a tourist destination, but what I hadn't realized was how crowded it had become at almost all hours of the day. There are several factors that make the *Sri Harmandir Sahib* (literally, "Abode of God") unique. One immediately notices, for instance, that there are no security checkpoints for entering into the complex. No visible metal detectors, no frisking by armed guards, no restrictions of any kind on who may or may not enter the sacred grounds.

All that is required is to wear proper attire, going barefoot so as to cleanse one's feet before entering, and wearing a head covering. Sikhism was founded by Guru Nanak, who was born in the latter part of the 15th century and established a lineage of nine succeeding human gurus (from Guru Angad to Guru Gobind Singh). It was the tenth guru in the 18th century who proclaimed that the holy writings of six of the Sikh gurus along with selected writings from such Sants as Kabir, Namdev, and the Sufi mystic, Sheikh Farid, would serve as the "final and eternal living guru" for all followers of the Sikh religion.

Written in Gurmukhi script, the *Sri Guru Granth Sahib* is held in the highest respect by Sikhs worldwide since it contains the essence of their spiritual philosophy. The book is housed in the innermost sanctum of the Golden Temple and is recited daily and is treated with the utmost care. Our driver, with the very apt and accurate name of "Happy", wanted my family and I to have a glimpse of the inner sanctum of the *Sri Harmandir Sahib*, even though it was just after 10 p.m. at night when a palanquin (known as the *Palki Sahib*) carries the sacred holy book of the Sikhs, the *Sri Guru Granth Sahib* to the *Akal*

Takhat Sahib. At this time, visitors (especially foreigners) are discouraged from entering the temple since devotees clean the *Sri Harmandir Sahib* for an hour or so. Fortunately, however, due to "Happy's" persistence we were allowed to witness the diligent work of these Sikh sevadars as they sang in the most intense and enchanting way the *Gurbani Kirtan*. I cannot even begin to describe how completely engaged and sincere the many *sevadars* were in doing the cleaning. It wasn't perfunctory in the least, but rather seen as a great honor to be able to do such work.

And one could palpably feel the energy, the excitement, and the yearning underlying the devotional singing. It was a surreal scene, the likes of which I will never forget. Although I was raised as a Roman Catholic, it was impossible not to be transfixed by the magnificence of the Golden Temple, but even more by the earnest love and devotion I personally saw among the vast throng who felt blessed by being able to glimpse their beloved guru. Coming home, late that night, I realized anew that what makes something sacred or numinous is the earnest desire of humans for that which transcends them.

While I am sure there is a better description for what I witnessed, somehow the phrase "Devotional Thickness" rung true. It is a human product and as such can illuminate and shine forth at anytime, anywhere, and at any place. It is not restricted to any particular ism and because of this, it can manifest unexpectedly. Of course, some places and some gatherings tend to bring out the very best in us and because of such, they become "sacred". The sanctity is not necessarily geographical (though that too does play a part), but rather part and parcel of our biological (and biographical) make-up.

Bring the deepest yearning in a human being to the forefront and you have the very best of spirituality, even if it is in a conference room filled with agnostics and atheists. What transforms is the human heart and what I saw at the Golden Temple was both simple and profound: a wide diversity of people bringing their "best" selves and their "deepest" aspirations. It makes perfect sense, regardless of one's religious affiliation (or lack thereof) to want to visit such communal centers of worship. As we all know, the world has far too many areas where humans bring their worst selves and act accordingly.

Even though there is much to criticize about religion, it is vitally important to remember that at certain times and in certain places unbounded human longing can be allowed to flourish and it is then and there that we can get a glimpse of the transcendent. This unique human quality, which in German is called *Sehnsucht* ("intensely missing"), can manifest wherever and whenever we acknowledge the mystery that both precedes and transcends us—whether it is a gathering of astronomers pondering the deepest reaches of the Milky Way or devoted Sikhs honoring the wisdom of their Gurus and their teachings.

The Golden Temple

Amritsar, Punjab, India

Sri Harmandir Sahib

ਸ੍ਰੀ ਹਰਮਿੰਦਰ ਸਾਹਬਿ

One Universal Creator
God.

The Name Is Truth.
Creative Being
Personified. No Fear.
No Hatred.

Image Of The Undying,
Beyond Birth, Self-
Existent. By Guru's
Grace ~

Chant And Meditate:

True In The Primal Beginning.

True Throughout The Ages.

True Here And Now.

O Nanak, Forever And Ever True.

3

By thinking, He cannot
be reduced to thought,
even by thinking
hundreds of thousands
of times.
By remaining silent,
inner silence is not
obtained, even by
remaining lovingly
absorbed
deep within.

The hunger of the hungry is not appeased, even by piling up loads of worldly goods. Hundreds of thousands of clever tricks, but not even one of them will go along with you in the end.

So how can you become truthful? And how can the veil of illusion be torn away? O Nanak, it is written that you shall obey the Hukam of His Command, and walk in the Way of His Will.

6

By His Command,
bodies are created; His
Command cannot be
described.
By His Command, souls
come into being; by His
Command, glory and
greatness are obtained.
By His Command, some
are high and some are
low; by His Written
Command, pain and
pleasure are obtained.

Some, by His Command, are blessed and forgiven; others, by His Command, wander aimlessly forever. Everyone is subject to His Command; no one is beyond His Command. O Nanak, one who understands His Command, does not speak in ego.

Some sing of His
Power-who has that
Power?

Some sing of His Gifts,
and know His Sign and
Insignia.

Some sing of His
Glorious Virtues,
Greatness and Beauty.

Some sing of knowledge obtained of Him, through difficult philosophical studies.

Some sing that He fashions the body, and then again reduces it to dust.

Some sing that He takes life away, and then again restores it.

10

Some sing that He
seems so very far away.

Some sing that He
watches over us, face to
face, ever-present.

11

There is no shortage of those who preach and teach.

Millions upon millions offer millions of sermons and stories.

The Great Giver keeps on giving, while those who receive grow weary of receiving.

Throughout the ages,
consumers consume.

The Commander, by
His Command, leads us
to walk on the Path.

O Nanak, He blossoms
forth, Carefree and
Untroubled.

True is the Master,
True is His Name-speak
it with infinite love.

People beg and pray,
"Give to us, give to us",
and the Great Giver
gives His Gifts.

So what offering can we
place before Him, by
which we might see the
Darbaar of His Court?

What words can we speak to evoke His Love?

In the *Amrit Vaylaa*, the ambrosial hours before dawn, chant the True Name, and contemplate His Glorious Greatness.

By the karma of past actions, the robe of this physical body is obtained. By His Grace, the Gate of Liberation is found.

O Nanak, know this well: the True One Himself is All.

He cannot be
established, He cannot
be created.

He Himself is
Immaculate and Pure.

Those who serve Him
are honored.

O Nanak, sing of the Lord, the Treasure of Excellence.

Sing, and listen, and let your mind be filled with love.

Your pain shall be sent far away, and peace shall come to your home.

The Guru's Word is the Sound-current of the Naad; the Guru's Word is the Wisdom of the Vedas; the Guru's Word is all-pervading.

The Guru is Shiva, the Guru is Vishnu and Brahma; the Guru is Paarvati and Lakhshmi.

Even knowing God, I cannot describe Him; He cannot be described in words.

The Guru has given me this one understanding: there is only the One, the Giver of all souls. May I never forget Him!

20

If I am pleasing to Him, then that is my pilgrimage and cleansing bath. Without pleasing Him, what good are ritual cleansings?

I gaze upon all the created beings: without the karma of good actions, what are they given to receive?

ਜਪੁਜੀ ਸਾਹਬਿ

Within the mind are gems, jewels and rubies, if you listen to the Guru's Teachings, even once.

The Guru has given me this one understanding: there is only the One, the Giver of all souls. May I never forget Him!

Even if you could live throughout the four ages, or even ten times more, and even if you were known throughout the nine continents and followed by all, with a good name and reputation, with praise and fame throughout the world-still, if the Lord does not bless you with His Glance of Grace, then who cares?

What is the use?

Among worms, you would be considered a lowly worm, and even contemptible sinners would hold you in contempt.

O Nanak, God blesses the unworthy with virtue, and bestows virtue on the virtuous.

No one can even
imagine anyone who can
bestow virtue upon Him.

Listening-the Siddhas,
the spiritual teachers,
the heroic warriors, the
yogic masters.

Listening-the earth, its
support and the
Akaashic ethers.

Listening-the oceans,
the lands of the world
and the nether regions
of the underworld.

Listening-Death cannot
even touch you.

O Nanak, the devotees
are forever in bliss.

Listening--pain and sin
are erased.

Listening--Shiva,
Brahma and Indra.

Listening--even foul-
mouthed people praise
Him.

Listening--the
technology of Yoga and
the secrets of the body.

Listening--the
Shaastras, the Simritees
and the Vedas.

O Nanak, the devotees
are forever in bliss.

Listening--pain and sin are erased.

Listening--truth, contentment and spiritual wisdom.

Listening--take your cleansing bath at the sixty-eight places of pilgrimage.

Listening--reading and
reciting, honor is
obtained.

Listening--intuitively
grasp the essence of
meditation.

O Nanak, the devotees
are forever in bliss.

Listening--pain and sin are erased.

Listening--dive deep into the ocean of virtue.

Listening--the Shaykhs, religious scholars, spiritual teachers and emperors.

Listening-even the blind
find the Path.

Listening-the
Unreachable comes
within your grasp.

O Nanak, the devotees
are forever in bliss.

Listening--pain and sin
are erased.

The state of the faithful
cannot be described.

One who tries to
describe this shall regret
the attempt.

No paper, no pen, no
scribe can record the
state of the faithful.

Such is the Name of the
Immaculate Lord.

Only one who has faith
comes to know such a
state of mind.

The faithful have
intuitive awareness and
intelligence.

The faithful know about
all worlds and realms.

The faithful shall never
be struck across the
face.

The faithful do not have to go with the Messenger of Death.

Such is the Name of the Immaculate Lord.

Only one who has faith comes to know such a state of mind.

The path of the faithful
shall never be blocked.

The faithful shall depart
with honor and fame.

The faithful do not
follow empty religious
rituals.

The faithful are firmly bound to the Dharma.

Such is the Name of the Immaculate Lord.

Only one who has faith comes to know such a state of mind.

The faithful find the
Door of Liberation.

The faithful uplift and
redeem their family and
relations.

The faithful are saved,
and carried across with
the Sikhs of the Guru.

The faithful, O Nanak,
do not wander around
begging.

Such is the Name of the
Immaculate Lord.

Only one who has faith
comes to know such a
state of mind.

The chosen ones, the self-elect, are accepted and approved.

The chosen ones are honored in the Court of the Lord.

The chosen ones look beautiful in the courts of kings.

The chosen ones
meditate single-
mindedly on the Guru.

No matter how much
anyone tries to explain
and describe them, the
actions of the Creator
cannot be counted.

The mythical bull is
Dharma, the son of
compassion; this is what
patiently holds the earth
in its place.

One who understands
this becomes truthful.

What a great load there
is on the bull!

So many worlds beyond
this world-so very many!

What power holds them,
and supports their
weight?

The names and the
colors of the assorted
species of beings were
all inscribed by the
Ever-flowing Pen of
God.

Who knows how to
write this account?

Just imagine what a
huge scroll it would
take!

What power! What
fascinating beauty!

And what gifts! Who can know their extent?

You created the vast expanse of the Universe with One Word!

Hundreds of thousands of rivers began to flow.

How can Your Creative Potency be described?

I cannot even once be a sacrifice to You.

Whatever pleases You is the only good done, You, Eternal and Formless One!

Countless meditations,
countless loves.

Countless worship
services, countless
austere disciplines.

Countless scriptures,
and ritual recitations of
the Vedas.

Countless Yogis, whose minds remain detached from the world.

Countless devotees contemplate the Wisdom and Virtues of the Lord.

Countless the holy, countless the givers.

Countless heroic spiritual warriors, who bear the brunt of the attack in battle (who with their mouths eat steel).

Countless silent sages, vibrating the String of His Love.

How can Your Creative Potency be described?

I cannot even once be a
sacrifice to You.

Whatever pleases You is
the only good done,

You, Eternal and
Formless One.

Countless fools, blinded
by ignorance.

Countless thieves and
embezzlers.

Countless impose their
will by force.

Countless cut-throats
and ruthless killers.

Countless sinners who
keep on sinning.

.

Countless liars,
wandering lost in their
lies.

Countless wretches,
eating filth as their
ration.

Countless slanderers,
carrying the weight of
their stupid mistakes on
their heads.

Nanak describes the
state of the lowly.
I cannot even once be a
sacrifice to You.

Whatever pleases You is
the only good done,
.
You, Eternal and
Formless One.

Countless names,
countless places.

Inaccessible,
unapproachable,
countless celestial
realms.

Even to call them
countless is to carry the
weight on your head.

From the Word, comes
the Naam; from the
Word, comes Your
Praise.

From the Word, comes
spiritual wisdom,
singing the Songs of
Your Glory.

.

From the Word, come
the written and spoken
words and hymns.

From the Word, comes
destiny, written on one's
forehead.

But the One who wrote
these Words of Destiny-
no words are written on
His Forehead.

As He ordains, so do we
receive.

The created universe is
the manifestation of
Your Name.

Without Your Name,
there is no place at all.

How can I describe Your Creative Power?

I cannot even once be a sacrifice to You.

Whatever pleases You is the only good done, You, Eternal and Formless One.

When the hands and the feet and the body are dirty, water can wash away the dirt.

When the clothes are soiled and stained by urine soap can wash them clean.

But when the intellect is stained and polluted by sin, it can only be cleansed by the Love of the Name.

Virtue and vice do not
come by mere words;
actions repeated, over
and over again, are
engraved on the soul.

You shall harvest what
you plant.

O Nanak, by the Hukam
of God's Command, we
come and go in
reincarnation.

Pilgrimages, austere
discipline, compassion
and charity--these, by
themselves, bring only
an iota of merit.

Listening and believing
with love and humility
in your mind, cleanse
yourself with the Name,
at the sacred shrine
deep within.

All virtues are Yours,
Lord, I have none at all.

Without virtue, there is
no devotional worship.

I bow to the Lord of the
World, to His Word, to
Brahma the Creator.

He is Beautiful, True
and Eternally Joyful.

What was that time, and
what was that moment?
What was that day, and
what was that date?

What was that season,
and what was that
month, when the
Universe was created?

The Pandits, the
religious scholars,
cannot find that time,
even if it is written in
the Puraanas.

That time is not known
to the Qazis, who study
the Koran.

The day and the date are
not known to the Yogis,
nor is the month or the
season.

The Creator who created this creation-only He Himself knows.

.

How can we speak of Him? How can we praise Him? How can we describe Him? How can we know Him?

O Nanak, everyone speaks of Him, each one wiser than the rest.

Great is the Master,
Great is His Name.
Whatever happens is
according to His Will.

O Nanak, one who
claims to know
everything shall not be
decorated in the world
hereafter.

There are nether worlds
beneath nether worlds,
and hundreds of
thousands of heavenly
worlds above.

The Vedas say that you
can search and search
for them all, until you
grow weary.

.

The scriptures say that there are 18,000 worlds, but in reality, there is only One Universe.

If you try to write an account of this, you will surely finish yourself before you finish writing it.

O Nanak, call Him Great! He Himself knows Himself.

The praisers praise the Lord, but they do not obtain intuitive understanding--the streams and rivers flowing into the ocean do not know its vastness.

Even kings and
emperors, with
mountains of property
and oceans of wealth--
these are not even equal
to an ant, who does not
forget God.

Endless are His Praises,
endless are those who
speak them.

Endless are His Actions,
endless are His Gifts.

Endless is His Vision,
endless is His Hearing.

His limits cannot be
perceived. What is the
Mystery of His Mind?

The limits of the created
universe cannot be
perceived.

Its limits here and
beyond cannot be
perceived.

Many struggle to know
His limits, but His limits
cannot be found.

No one can know these limits.

The more you say about them, the more there still remains to be said.

Great is the Master, High is His Heavenly Home.

Highest of the High, above all is His Name.

Only one as Great and as High as God can know His Lofty and Exalted State.

Only He Himself is that Great. He Himself knows Himself.

O Nanak, by His Glance of Grace, He bestows His Blessings.

His Blessings are so abundant that there can be no written account of them.

The Great Giver does not hold back anything.

There are so many great, heroic warriors begging at the Door of the Infinite Lord.

So many contemplate
and dwell upon Him,
that they cannot be
counted.

So many waste away to
death engaged in
corruption.

So many take and take
again, and then deny
receiving.

So many foolish
consumers keep on
consuming.

So many endure
distress, deprivation and
constant abuse.

Even these are Your
Gifts, O Great Giver!

Liberation from
bondage comes only by
Your Will.

No one else has any say in this.

If some fool should presume to say that he does,

he shall learn, and feel the effects of his folly.

He Himself knows, He Himself gives.

Few, very few are those who acknowledge this.

One who is blessed to sing the Praises of the Lord, O Nanak, is the king of kings.

Priceless are His Virtues, Priceless are His Dealings.

Priceless are His
Dealers, Priceless are
His Treasures.

Priceless are those who
come to Him, Priceless
are those who buy from
Him.

Priceless is Love for
Him, Priceless is
absorption into Him.

Priceless is the Divine
Law of Dharma,
Priceless is the Divine
Court of Justice.

Priceless are the scales,
priceless are the
weights.

Priceless are His
Blessings, Priceless is
His Banner and Insignia.

Priceless, O Priceless beyond expression!

Speak of Him continually, and remain absorbed in His Love.

The Vedas and the Puraanas speak.

The scholars speak and lecture.

Brahma speaks, Indra
speaks.

The Gopis and Krishna
speak.

Shiva speaks, the
Siddhas speak.

The many created
Buddhas speak.

The demons speak, the demi-gods speak.

The spiritual warriors, the heavenly beings, the silent sages, the humble and serviceful speak.

Many speak and try to describe Him.

Many have spoken of Him over and over again, and have then arisen and departed.

If He were to create as many again as there already are, even then, they could not describe Him.

He is as Great as He wishes to be.

O Nanak, the True Lord knows.

If anyone presumes to describe God, he shall be known as the greatest fool of fools!

Where is that Gate, and
where is that Dwelling,
in which You sit and
take care of all?

The Sound-current of
the Naad vibrates there,
and countless musicians
play on all sorts of
instruments there.

So many Ragas, so many musicians singing there.

The praanic wind, water and fire sing; the Righteous Judge of Dharma sings at Your Door. record sing.

Chitr and Gupt, the angels of the conscious and the subconscious who record actions, and the Righteous Judge of Dharma who judges this record sing.

Shiva, Brahma and the Goddess of Beauty, ever adorned, sing.

Indra, seated upon His Throne, sings with the deities at Your Door.

The Siddhas in Samaadhi sing; the Saadhus sing in contemplation.

The celibates, the fanatics, the peacefully accepting and the fearless warriors sing.

The Pandits, the religious scholars who recite the Vedas, with the supreme sages of all the ages, sing.

The Mohinis, the enchanting heavenly beauties who entice hearts in this world, in paradise, and in the underworld of the subconscious sing.

The celestial jewels created by You, and the sixty-eight holy places of pilgrimage sing.

The brave and mighty warriors sing; the spiritual heroes and the four sources of creation sing.

The planets, solar systems and galaxies, created and arranged by Your Hand, sing.

They alone sing, who are pleasing to Your Will. Your devotees are imbued with the Nectar of Your Essence.

So many others sing, they do not come to mind. O Nanak, how can I consider them all?

That True Lord is True, Forever True, and True is His Name.

He is, and shall always be. He shall not depart, even when this Universe which He has created departs.

He created the world, with its various colors, species of beings, and the variety of Maya.

Having created the creation, He watches over it Himself, by His Greatness.

He does whatever He pleases. No order can be issued to Him.

He is the King, the King of kings, the Supreme Lord and Master of kings. Nanak remains subject to His Will.

Make contentment your ear-rings, humility your begging bowl, and meditation the ashes you apply to your body.

Let the remembrance of death be the patched coat you wear, let the purity of virginity be your way in the world, and let faith in the Lord be your walking stick.

See the brotherhood of all mankind as the highest order of Yogis; conquer your own mind, and conquer the world.

I bow to Him, I humbly bow.

The Primal One, the Pure Light, without beginning, without end. Throughout all the ages, He is One and the Same.

Let spiritual wisdom be your food, and compassion your attendant. The Sound-current of the Naad vibrates in each and every heart.

He Himself is the
Supreme Master of all;
wealth and miraculous
spiritual powers, and all
other external tastes and
pleasures, are all like
beads on a string.

Union with Him, and
separation from Him,
come by His Will. We
come to receive what is
written in our destiny.

I bow to Him,
I humbly bow.

The Primal One, the
Pure Light, without
beginning, without end.
Throughout all the ages,
He is One and the
Same.

The One Divine Mother
conceived and gave birth
to the three deities.

One, the Creator of the
World; One, the
Sustainer; and One, the
Destroyer.

He makes things happen
according to the
Pleasure of His Will.
Such is His Celestial
Order.

He watches over all, but none see Him. How wonderful this is!

I bow to Him, I humbly bow.

The Primal One, the Pure Light, without beginning, without end. Throughout all the ages, He is One and the Same.

On world after world are
His Seats of Authority
and His Storehouses.

Whatever was put into
them, was put there
once and for all.

Having created the
creation, the Creator
Lord watches over it.

O Nanak, True is the Creation of the True Lord.

I bow to Him, I humbly bow.

The Primal One, the Pure Light, without beginning, without end. Throughout all the ages, He is One and the Same.

If I had 100,000 tongues,
and these were then
multiplied twenty times
more, with each tongue,

I would repeat,
hundreds of thousands
of times, the Name of
the One, the Lord of the
Universe.

Along this path to our Husband Lord, we climb the steps of the ladder, and come to merge with Him.

Hearing of the etheric realms, even worms long to come back home.

O Nanak, by His Grace He is obtained. False are the boastings of the false.

No power to speak, no
power to keep silent.

No power to beg, no
power to give.

No power to live, no
power to die.

No power to rule, with
wealth and occult
mental powers.

No power to gain intuitive understanding, spiritual wisdom and meditation.

No power to find the way to escape from the world.

He alone has the Power in His Hands. He watches over all.

O Nanak, no one is high or low.

Nights, days, weeks and seasons; wind, water, fire and the nether regions--in the midst of these, He established the earth as a home for Dharma.

Upon it, He placed the various species of beings.

Their names are uncounted and endless.

By their deeds and their actions, they shall be judged.

God Himself is True, and True is His Court.

There, in perfect grace
and ease, sit the self-
elect, the self-realized
Saints.

They receive the Mark of
Grace from the Merciful
Lord.

The ripe and the unripe,
the good and the bad,
shall there be judged.

O Nanak, when you go
home, you will see this.

This is righteous living
in the realm of Dharma.

And now we speak of
the realm of spiritual
wisdom.

So many winds, waters and fires; so many Krishnas and Shivas.

So many Brahmas, fashioning forms of great beauty, adorned and dressed in many colors.

So many worlds and lands for working out karma. So very many lessons to be learned!

So many Indras, so many moons and suns, so many worlds and lands. So many Siddhas and Buddhas, so many Yogic masters. So many goddesses of various kinds.

So many demi-gods and demons, so many silent sages. So many oceans of jewels.

So many ways of life, so many languages. So many dynasties of rulers.

So many intuitive people, so many selfless servants. O Nanak, His limit has no limit!

In the realm of wisdom, spiritual wisdom reigns supreme.

The Sound-current of
the Naad vibrates there,
amidst the sounds and
the sights of bliss.

In the realm of humility,
the Word is Beauty.

Forms of incomparable
beauty are fashioned
there.

These things cannot be
described.

One who tries to speak
of these shall regret the
attempt.

The intuitive consciousness, intellect and understanding of the mind are shaped there. The consciousness of the spiritual warriors and the Siddhas, the beings of spiritual perfection, are shaped there. In the realm of karma, the Word is Power.

No one else dwells there,
except the warriors of
great power, the
spiritual heroes.

They are totally fulfilled,
imbued with the Lord's
Essence.

Myriads of Sitas are
there, cool and calm in
their majestic glory.

Their beauty cannot be
described.

Neither death nor
deception comes to
those, within whose
minds the Lord abides.

The devotees of many worlds dwell there.

They celebrate; their minds are imbued with the True Lord.

In the realm of Truth, the Formless Lord abides.

Having created the creation, He watches over it. By His Glance of Grace, He bestows happiness.

There are planets, solar systems and galaxies.

If one speaks of them, there is no limit, no end.

There are worlds upon worlds of His Creation.

As He commands, so they exist.

He watches over all, and contemplating the creation, He rejoices.

O Nanak, to describe
this is as hard as steel!

Let self-control be the
furnace, and patience
the goldsmith.

Let understanding be
the anvil, and spiritual
wisdom the tools.

With the Fear of God as the bellows, fan the flames of tapa, the body's inner heat.

In the crucible of love, melt the Nectar of the Name, and mint the True Coin of the Shabad, the Word of God.

Such is the karma of those upon whom He has cast His Glance of Grace.

O Nanak, the Merciful Lord, by His Grace, uplifts and exalts them.

Air is the Guru, Water is the Father, and Earth is the Great Mother of all.

Day and night are the two nurses, in whose lap all the world is at play.

Good deeds and bad deeds-the record is read out in the Presence of the Lord of Dharma.

According to their own actions, some are drawn closer, and some are driven farther away.

Those who have
meditated on the Naam,
the Name of the Lord,
and departed after
having worked by the
sweat of their brows--
O Nanak, their faces are
radiant in the Court of
the Lord, and many are
saved along with them!

Guru Nanak

ਜਪੁਜੀ ਸਾਹਿਬ

Manufactured by Amazon.ca
Bolton, ON

10976339R00088